HAL•LEONARD

BASS

PLAY-ALONG

AUDIO ACCESS INCLUDED

VOL. 50

JACO PASTORIUS

T0070911

PLAYBACK+
Speed • Pitch • Balance • Loop

To access audio visit:
www.halleonard.com/mylibrary

Enter Code
3574-2512-2340-6238

Cover photo: Paul Natkin

Recording credits:
Bass by Jon Liebman
Guitar by Louka Patenaude
All other instrumentation by Chris Romero

ISBN 978-1-4803-9244-1

HAL•LEONARD®
CORPORATION
7777 W. BLUEMOUND RD. P.O. BOX 13819 MILWAUKEE, WI 53213

Visit Hal Leonard Online at
www.halleonard.com

BASS NOTATION LEGEND

Bass music can be notated two different ways: on a *musical staff*, and in *tablature*

THE MUSICAL STAFF shows pitches and rhythms and is divided by bar lines into measures. Pitches are named after the first seven letters of the alphabet.

TABLATURE graphically represents the bass fingerboard. Each horizontal line represents a string, and each number represents a fret.

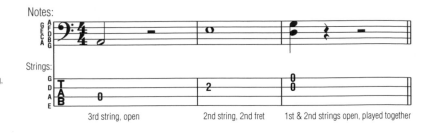

| 3rd string, open | 2nd string, 2nd fret | 1st & 2nd strings open, played together |

HAMMER-ON: Strike the first (lower) note with one finger, then sound the higher note (on the same string) with another finger by fretting it without picking.

PULL-OFF: Place both fingers on the notes to be sounded. Strike the first note and without picking, pull the finger off to sound the second (lower) note.

LEGATO SLIDE: Strike the first note and then slide the same fret-hand finger up or down to the second note. The second note is not struck.

SHIFT SLIDE: Same as legato slide, except the second note is struck.

TRILL: Very rapidly alternate between the notes indicated by continuously hammering on and pulling off.

TREMOLO PICKING: The note is picked as rapidly and continuously as possible.

VIBRATO: The string is vibrated by rapidly bending and releasing the note with the fretting hand.

SHAKE: Using one finger, rapidly alternate between two notes on one string by sliding either a half-step above or below.

NATURAL HARMONIC: Strike the note while the fret hand lightly touches the string directly over the fret indicated.

MUFFLED STRINGS: A percussive sound is produced by laying the fret hand across the string(s) without depressing them and striking them with the pick hand.

BEND: Strike the note and bend up the interval shown.

BEND AND RELEASE: Strike the note and bend up as indicated, then release back to the original note. Only the first note is struck.

RIGHT-HAND TAP: Hammer ("tap") the fret indicated with the "pick-hand" index or middle finger and pull off to the note fretted by the fret hand.

LEFT-HAND TAP: Hammer ("tap") the fret indicated with the "fret-hand" index or middle finger.

SLAP: Strike ("slap") string with right-hand thumb.

POP: Snap ("pop") string with right-hand index or middle finger.

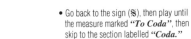

Additional Musical Definitions

 (accent) • Accentuate note (play it louder)

 (accent) • Accentuate note with great intensity

 (staccato) • Play the note short

D.S. al Coda • Go back to the sign (𝄋), then play until the measure marked *"To Coda"*, then skip to the section labelled *"Coda."*

Fill • Label used to identify a brief pattern which is to be inserted into the arrangement.

• Repeat measures between signs.

1. 2. • When a repeated section has different endings, play the first ending only the first time and the second ending only the second time.

CONTENTS

Birdland

By Josef Zawinul

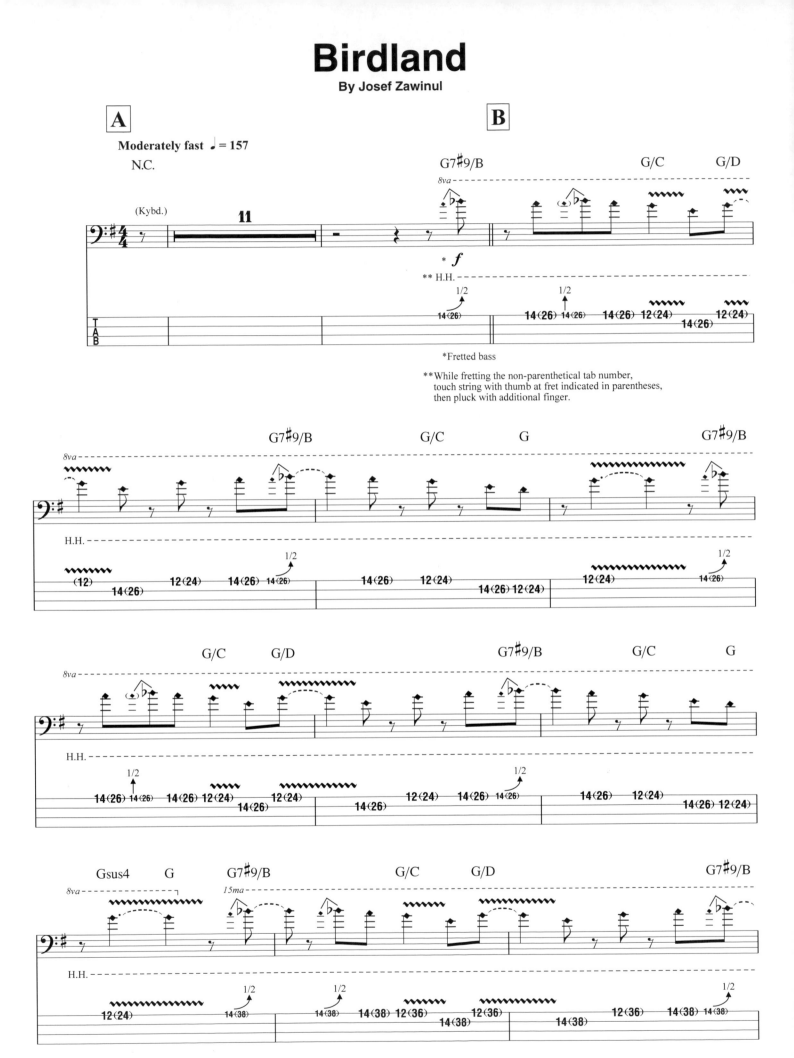

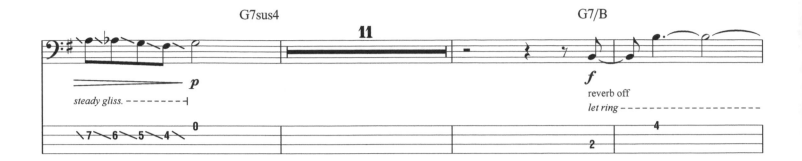

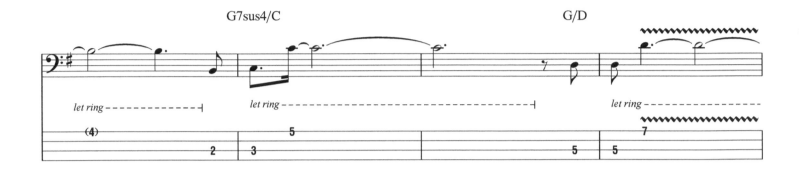

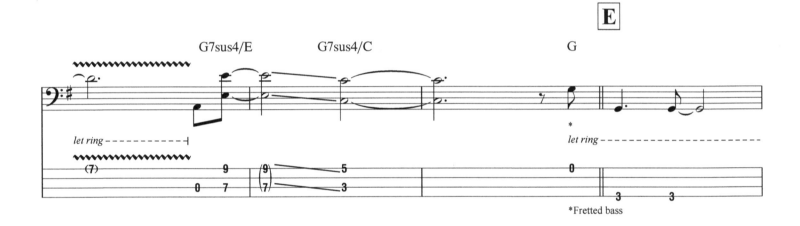

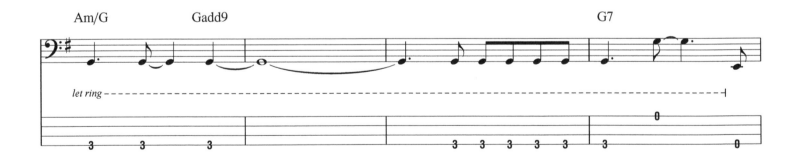

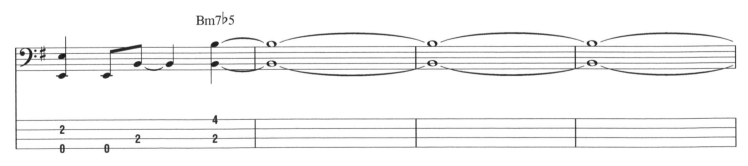

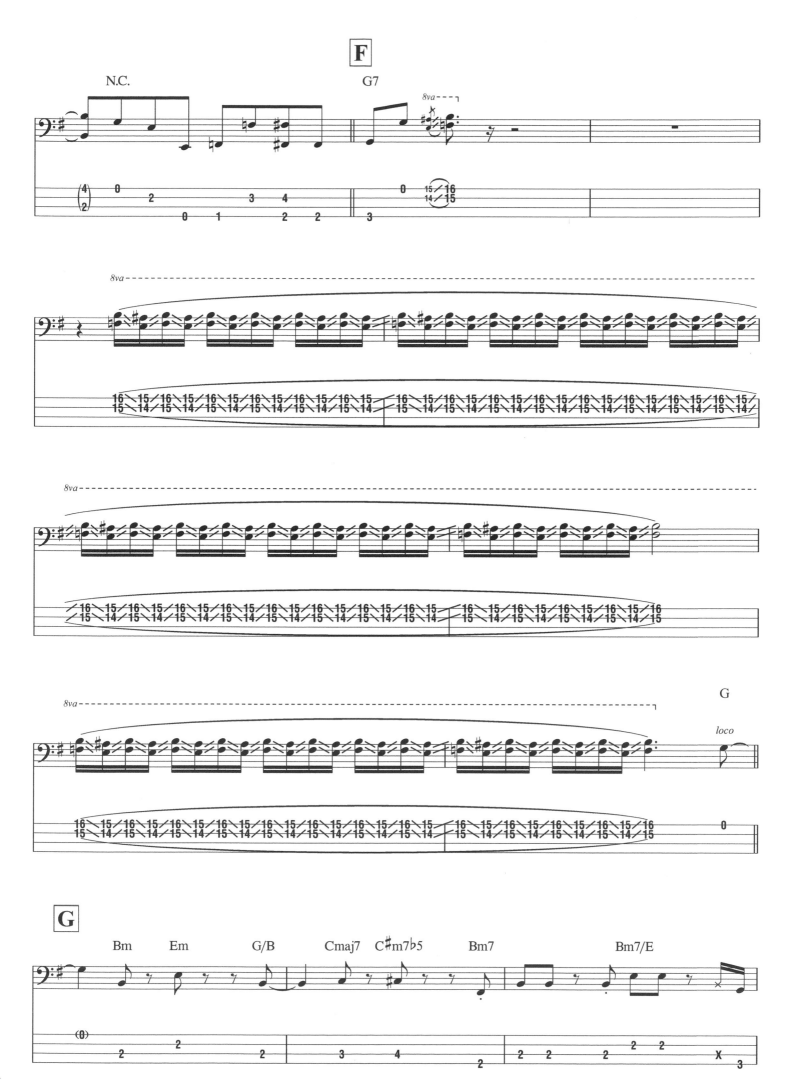

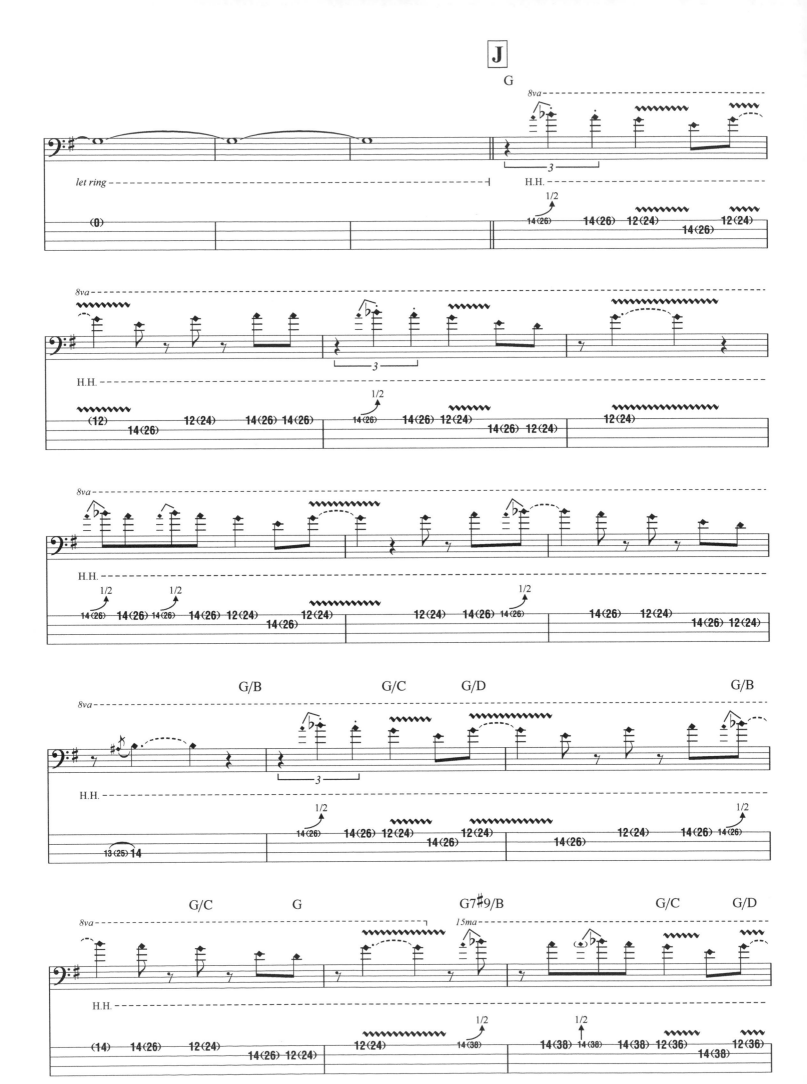

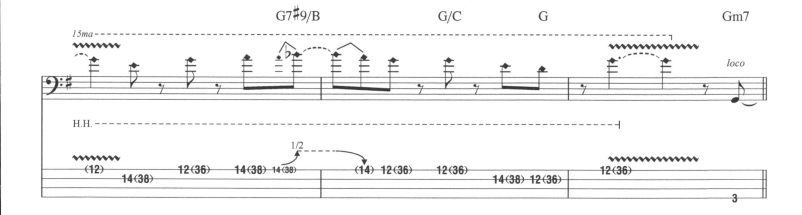

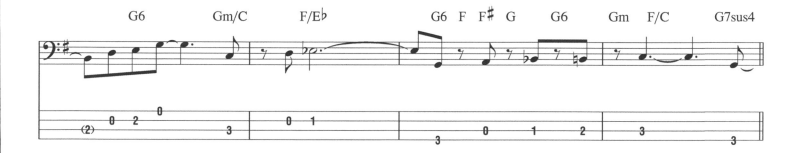

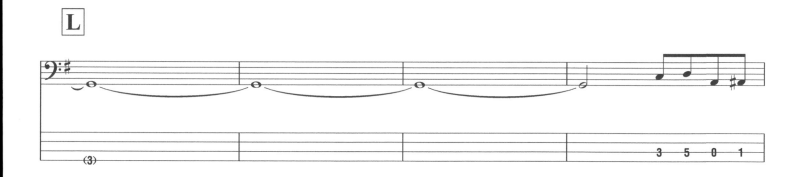

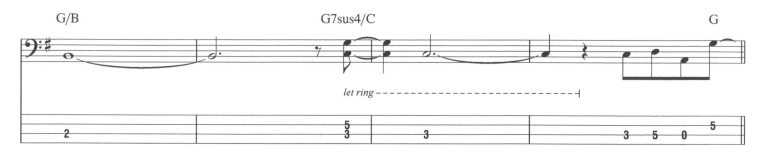

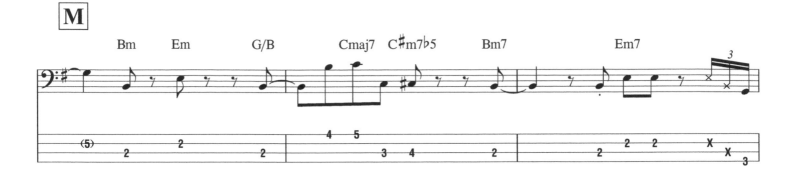

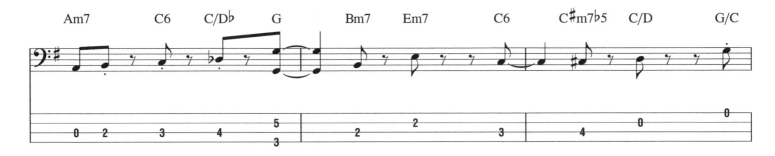

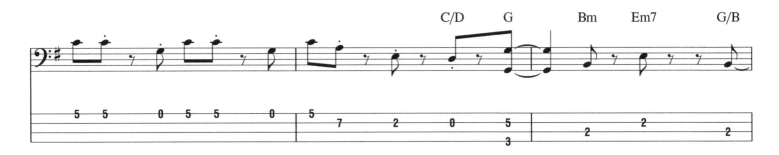

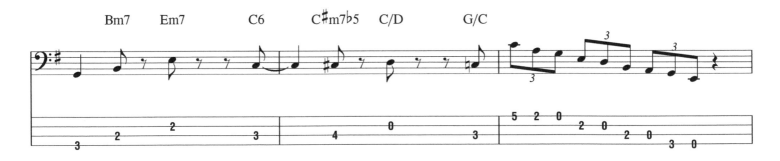

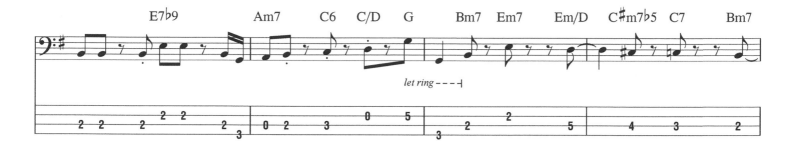

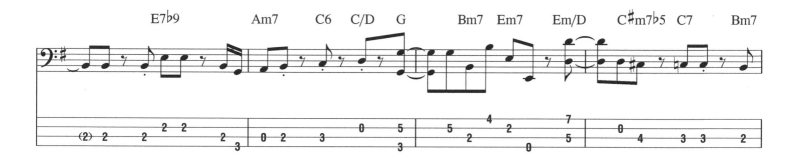

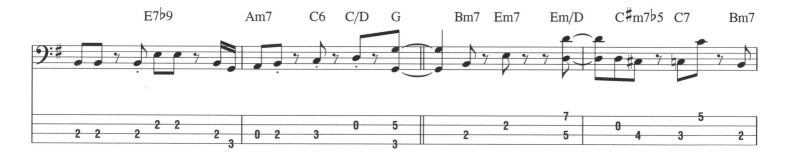

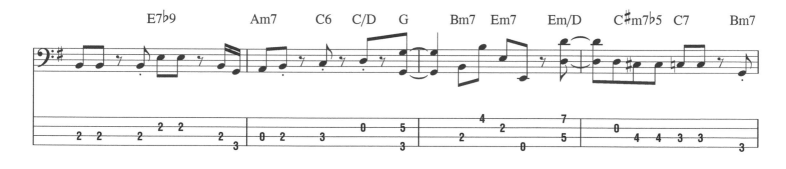

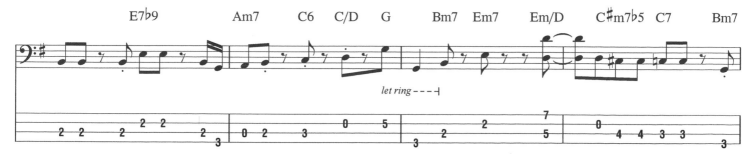

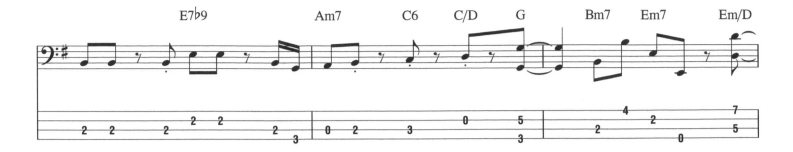

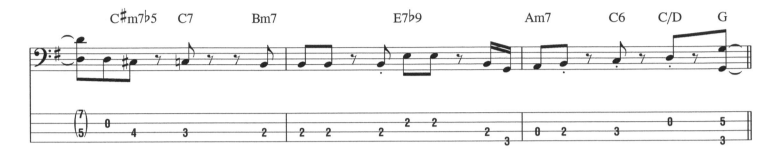

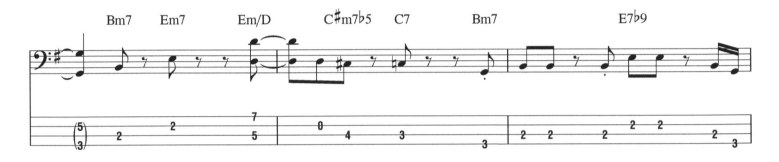

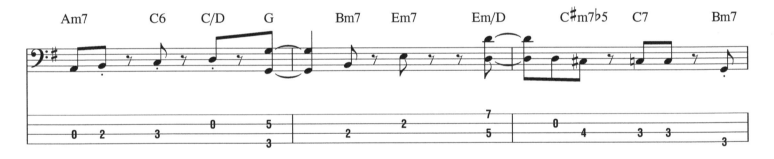

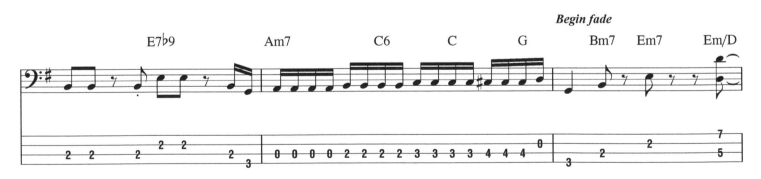

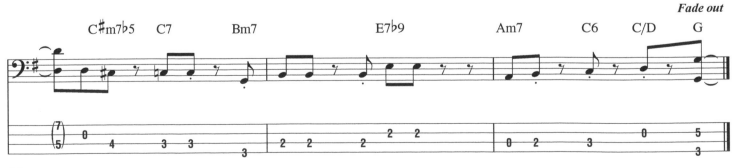

Come On, Come Over

By Jaco Pastorius and Bob Herzog

1. Come on, _____ come o - ver
2., 3. *See additional lyrics*

as fast as you can. _____

You're a - fraid ___ that you won't ___ like it,

but you don't un - der - stand. _____

One thing, _____ my bro - ther, _____

I can tell _____ you true: _____

The more time _____ you spend _____ feel - ing hap - py, the

To Coda 1 ⊕
To Coda 2 ⊕

C9   C#9

less time _ you'll be _____ blue. _____

Chorus

Come on, come on o - ver.

Come on, come on o - ver, ah.

Come on, ya got to come o - ver. Why don't you

come on, come on, come on o - ver?

Interlude

D.S. al Coda 1

Coda 1

Chorus

Come on, come on o - ver, _____ yeah. _____

Come on, _____ come on o - ver, _____ ah. _____ Why don't you

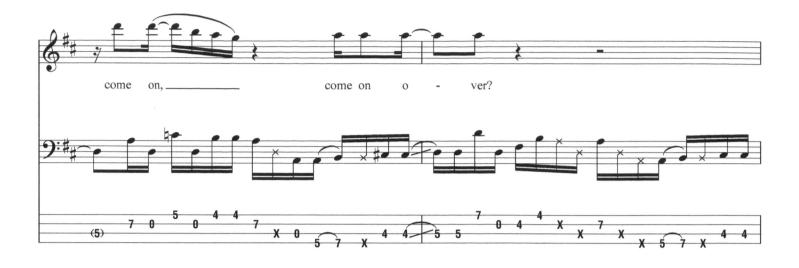

come on, _____ come on o - ver?

Come on, _____ oh, _____ come on o - ver, _____ yeah. _

Keyboard Solo

D9

F7

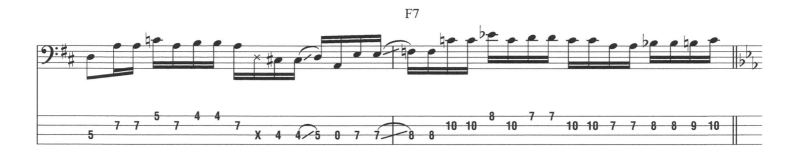

Interlude

Cm7

D.S. al Coda 2

 Coda 2

Outro-Chorus

D9

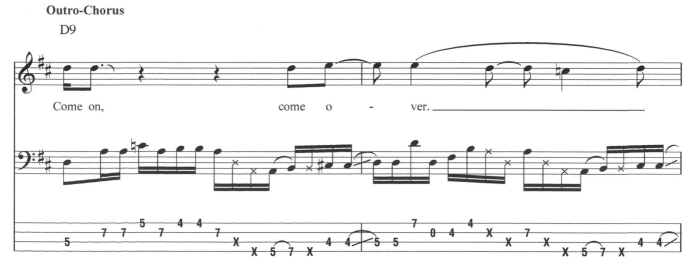

Come on,   come o - ver.

Come on,＿＿＿ come on o - ver. Don't＿ take＿＿＿

Begin fade

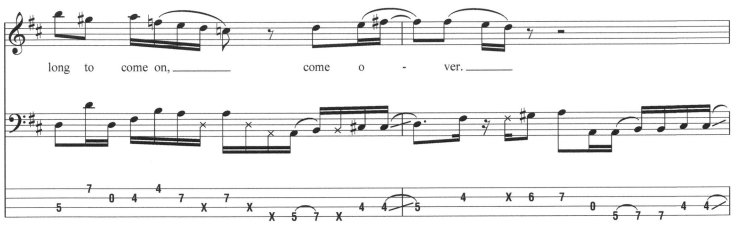

long to come on,＿＿＿ come o - ver.＿＿＿

Fade out

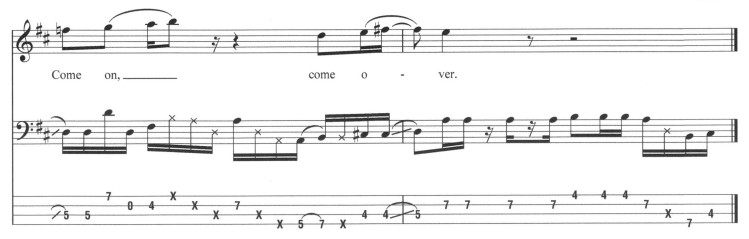

Come on,＿＿＿ come o - ver.

Additional Lyrics

2. Come on, come over. Ev'ryone's waitin' on you, yeah.
   We're wondering when you'll get tired of wondering what to do.
   There is somethin' here that cannot be denied.
   Get on the phone and get on down. Don't knock it till you try.

3. Come on, come over. The pleasure's all mine.
   Music playin', the door just opened. You don't have to stand in line.
   People of the world, ya been uptight, moving much too long.
   While you're busy makin' a stand, ev'rybody's makin' plans to move on, move 'em all along.

Bright Size Life

By Pat Metheny

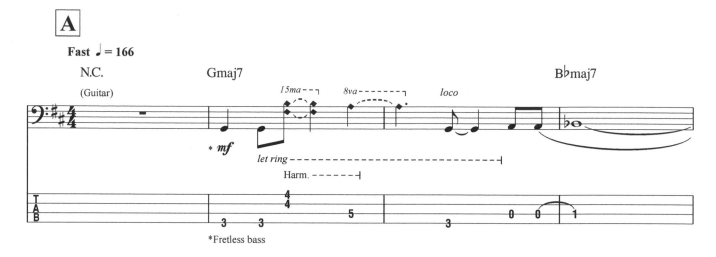

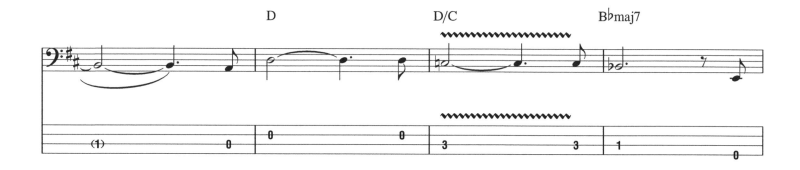

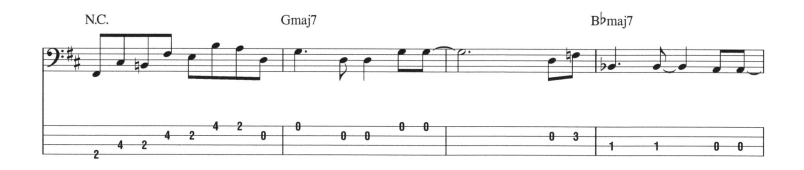

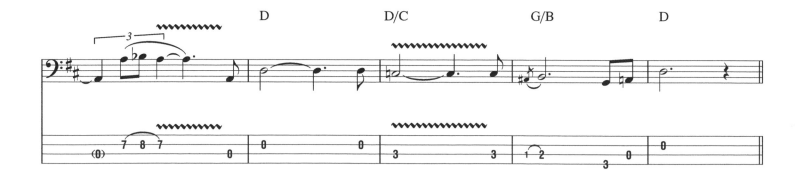

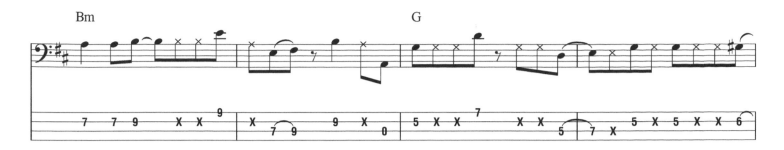

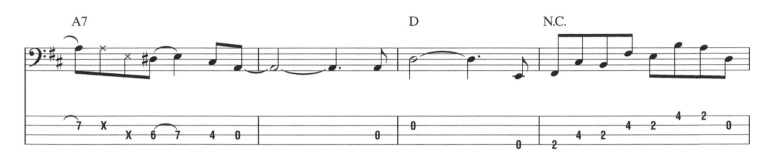

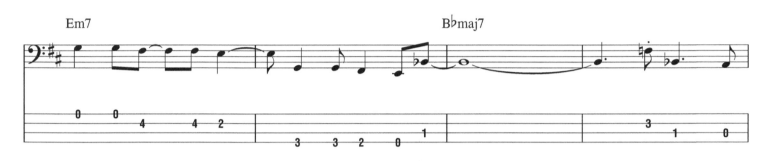

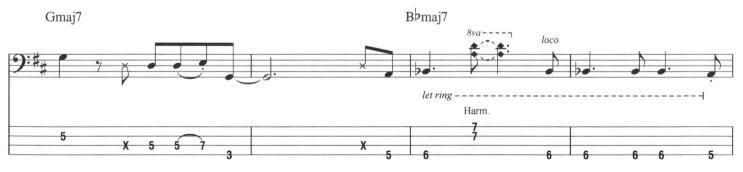

 B

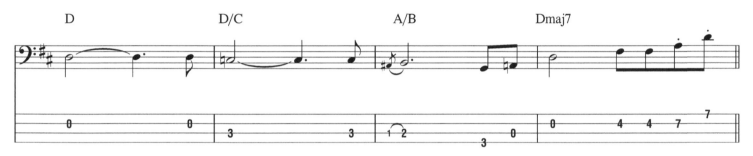

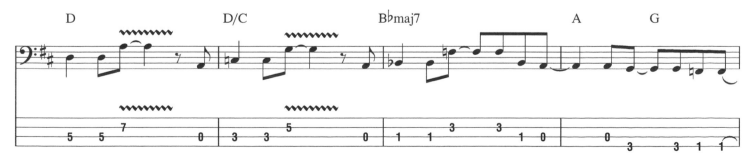

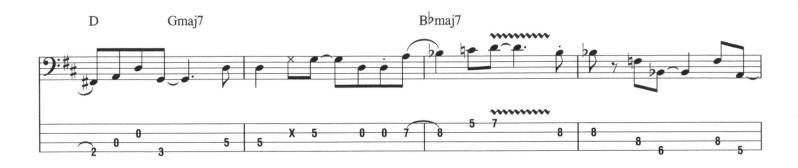

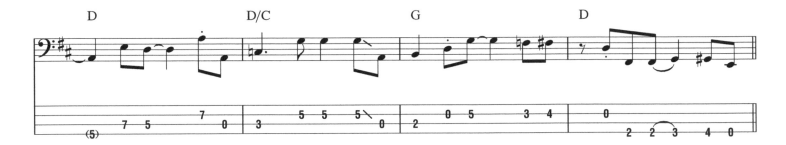

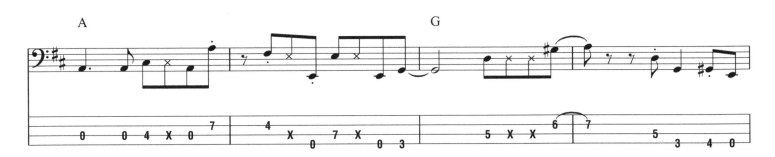

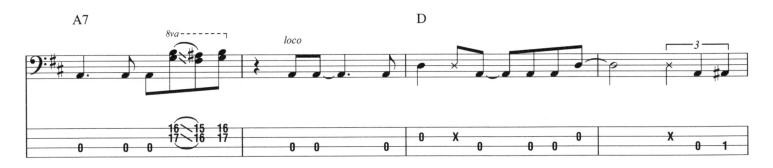

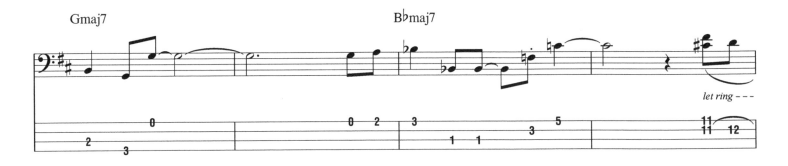

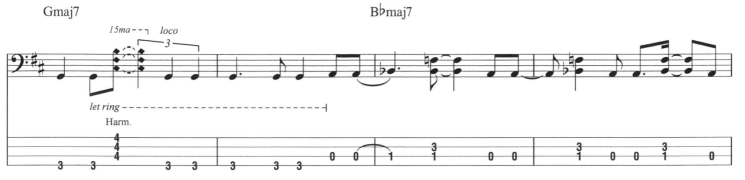

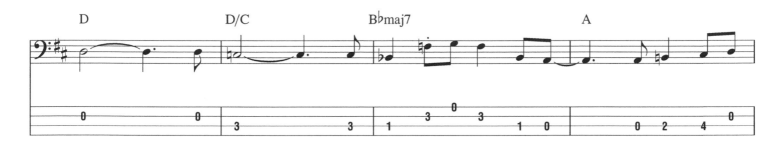

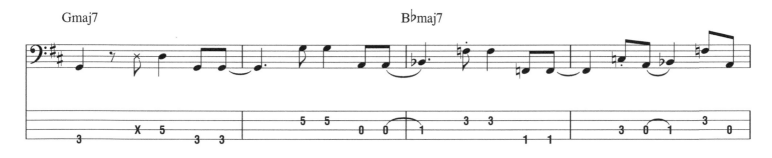

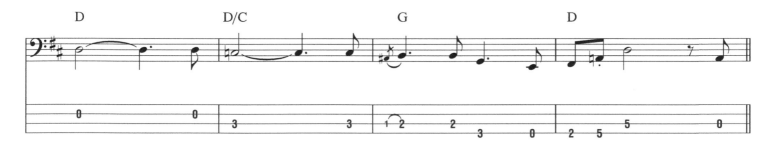

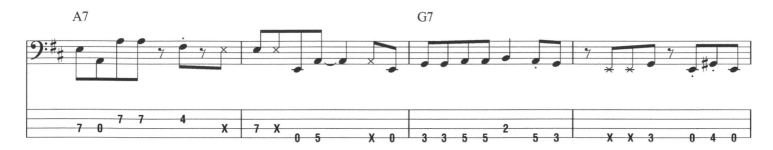

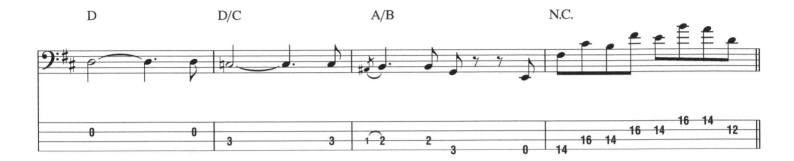

*Played behind the beat.

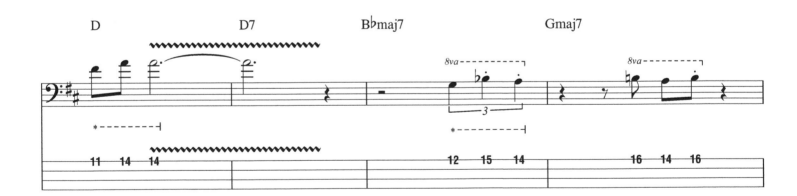

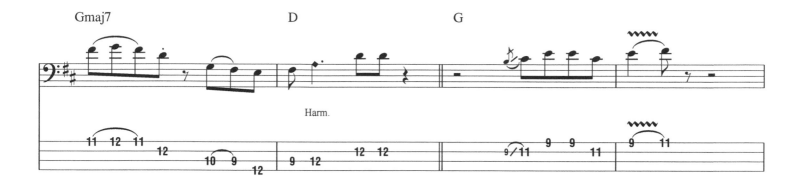

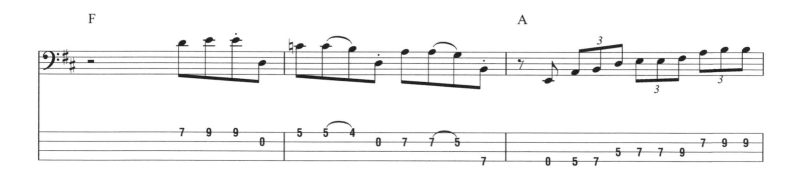

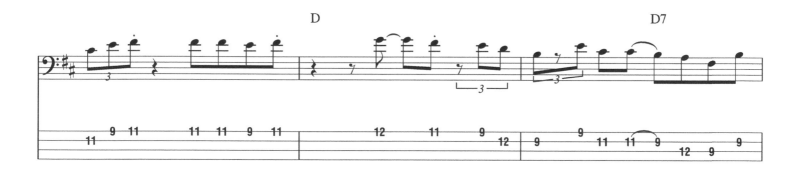

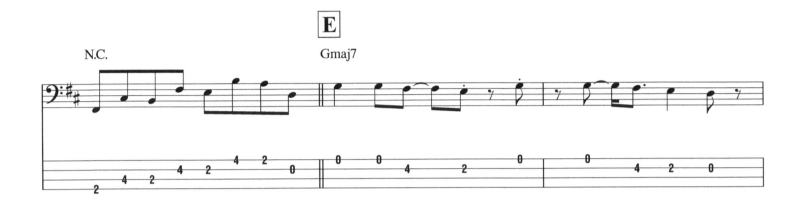

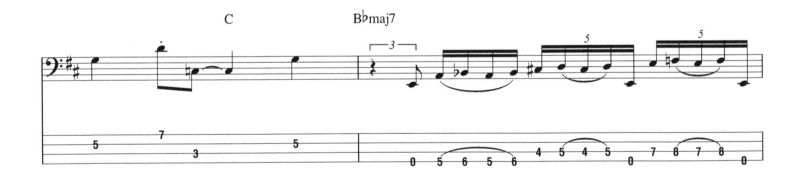

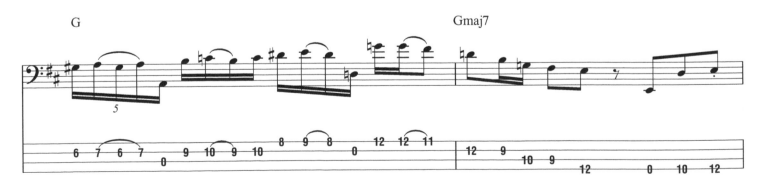

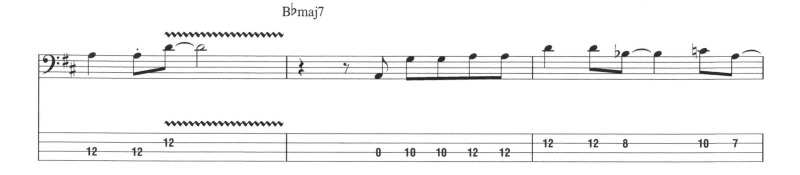

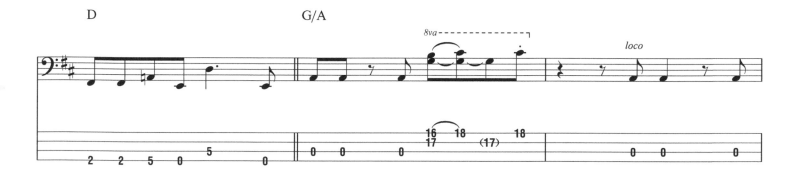

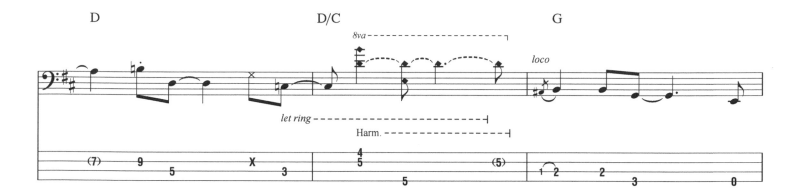

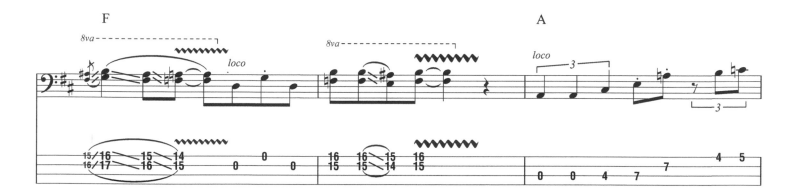

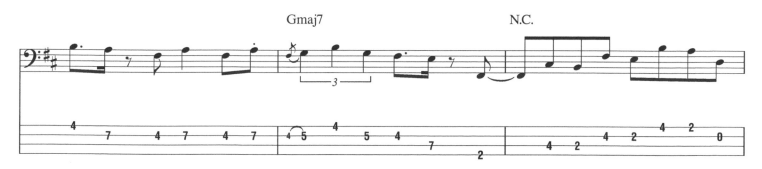

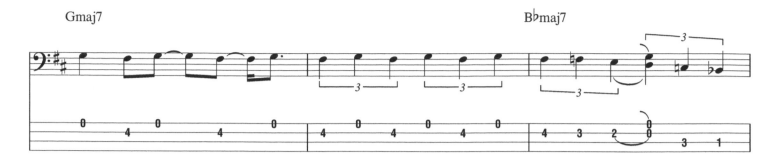

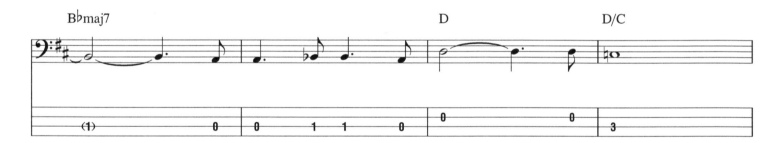

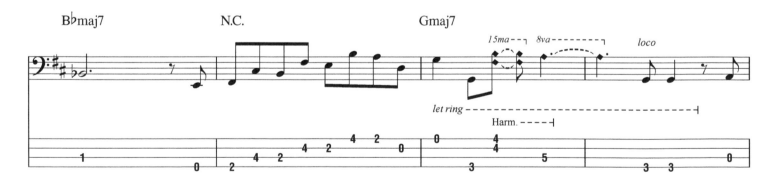

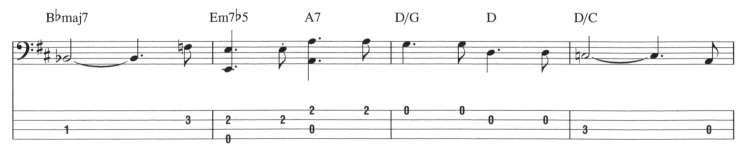

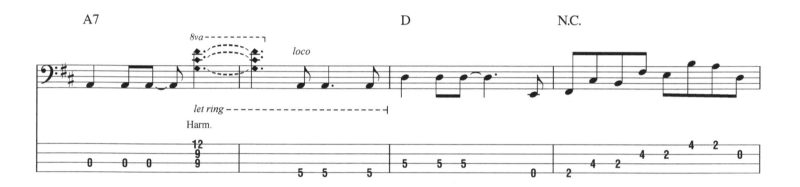

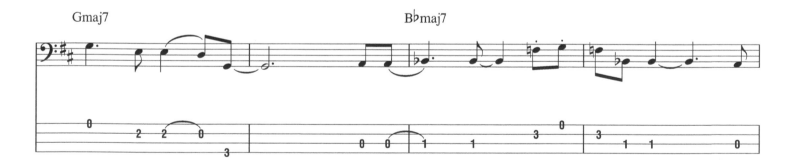

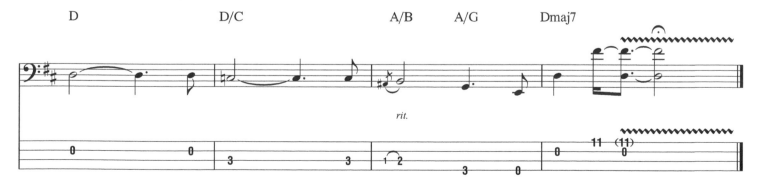

Continuum

By Jaco Pastorius

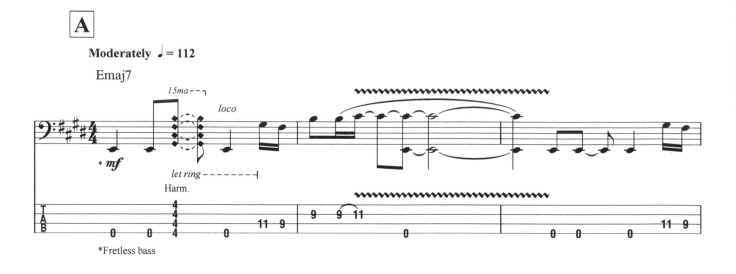

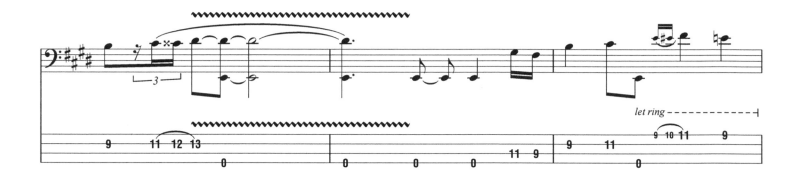

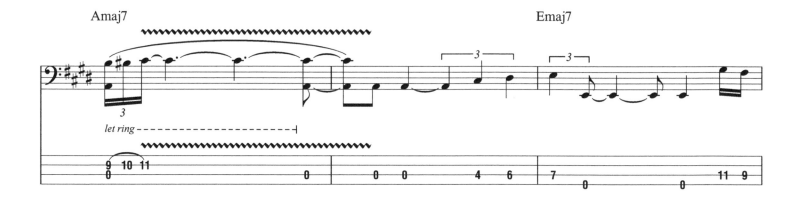

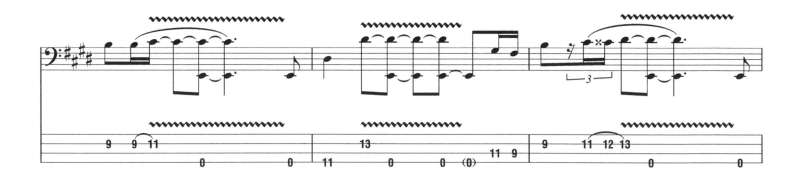

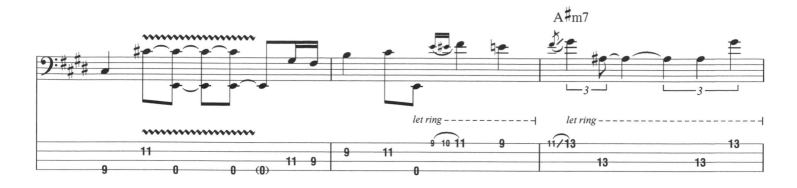

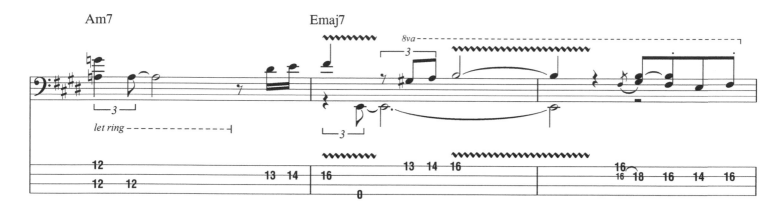

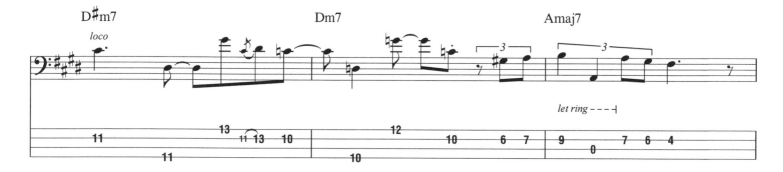

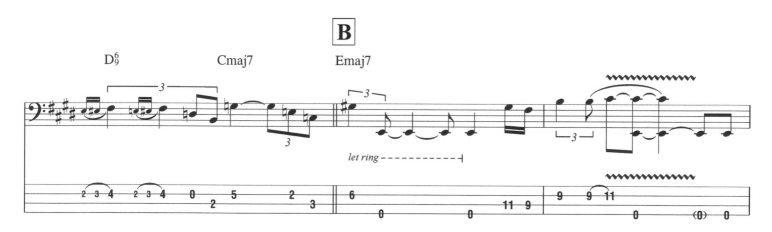

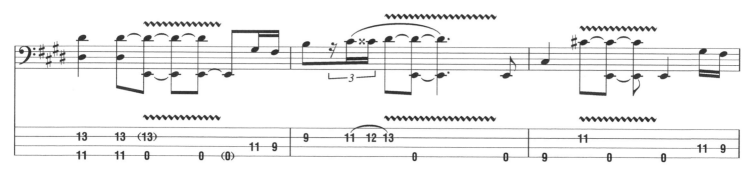

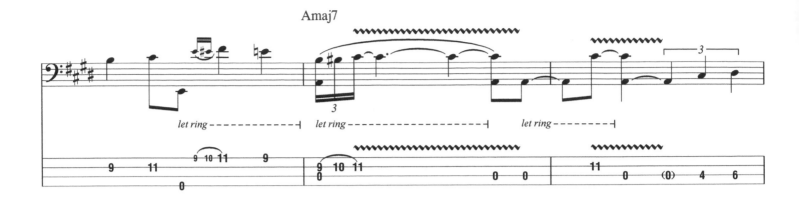

Amaj7

let ring

Emaj7

* 8va

loco

*Where two voices are present,
8va applies to upstemmed
notes only throughout.

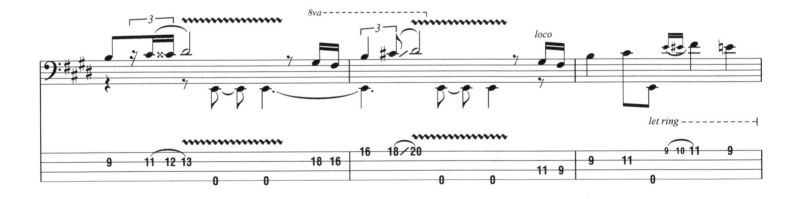

3
8va

loco

let ring

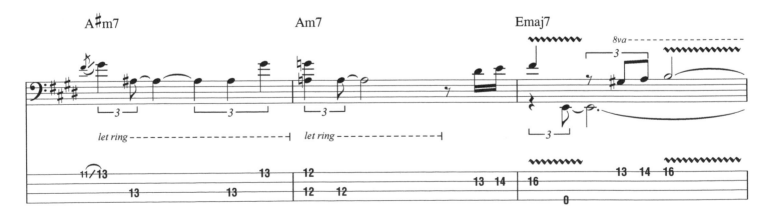

A♯m7   Am7   Emaj7

let ring   *let ring*

8va

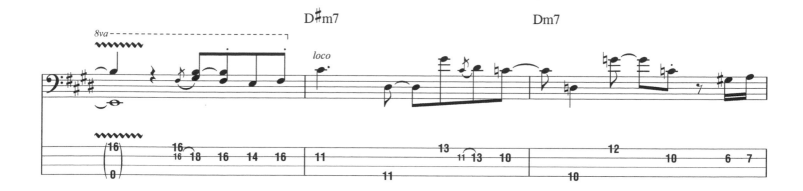

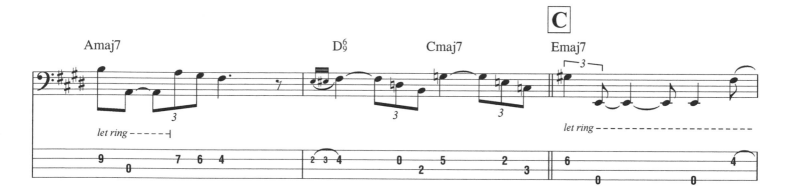

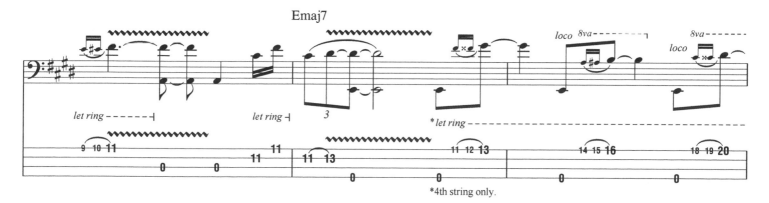

*4th string only.

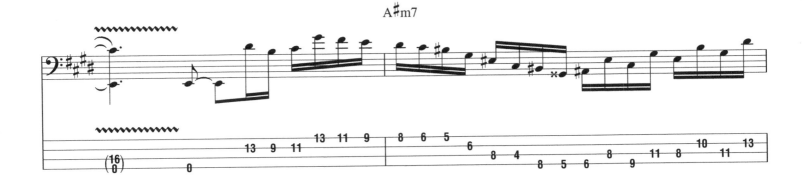

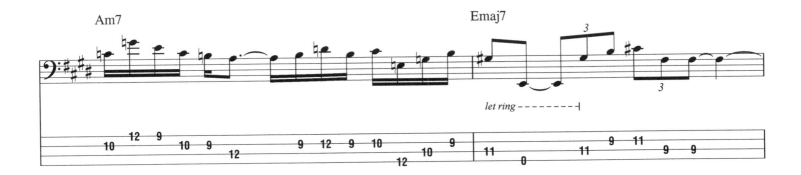

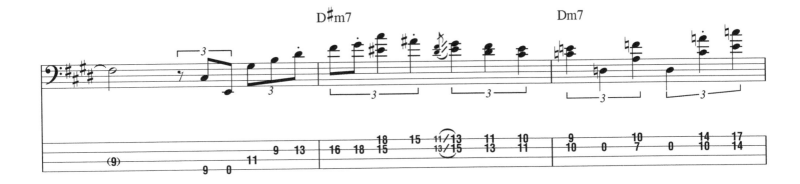

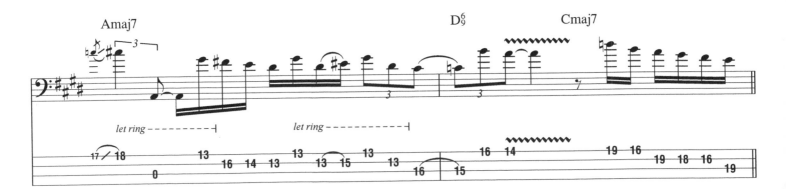

D

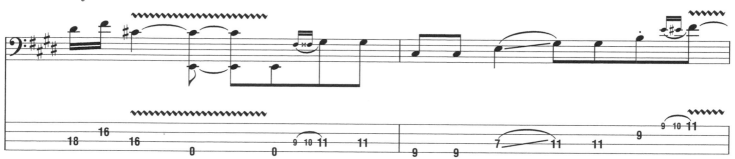

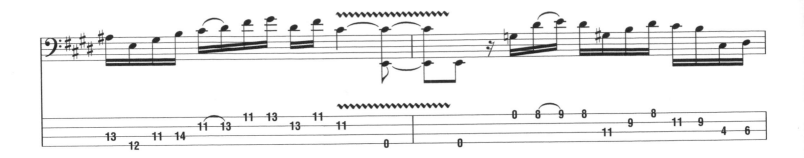

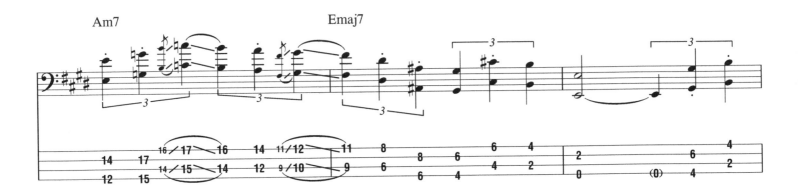

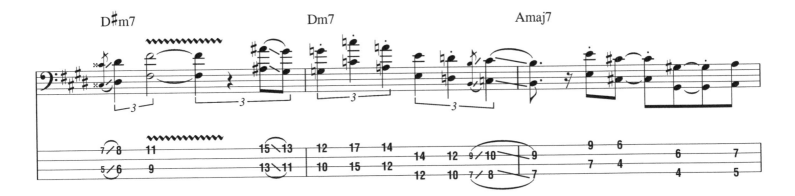

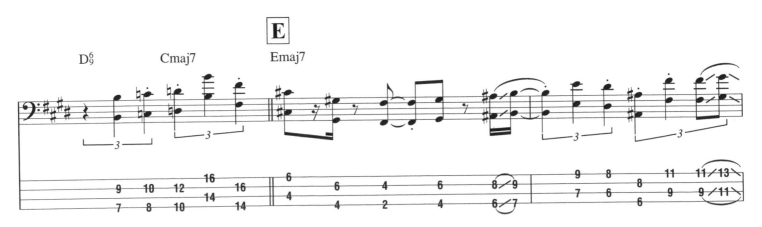

Amaj7

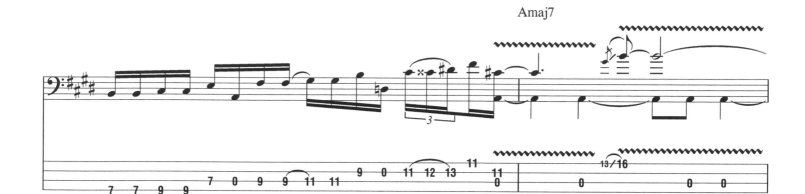

Emaj7

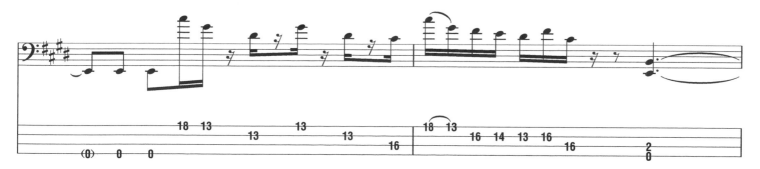

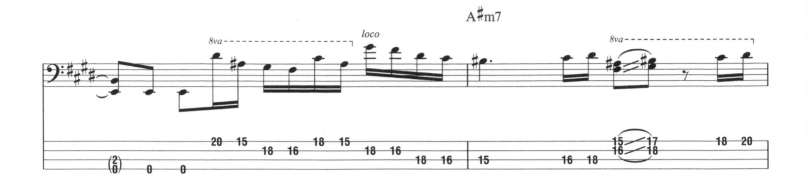

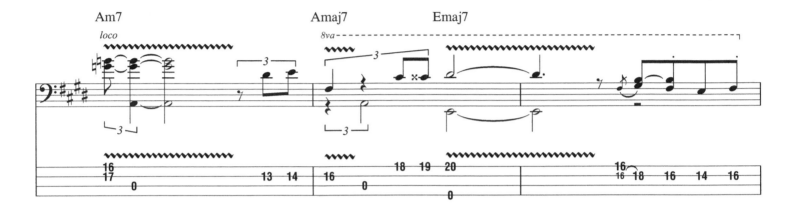

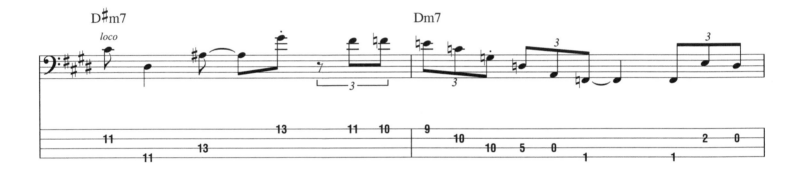

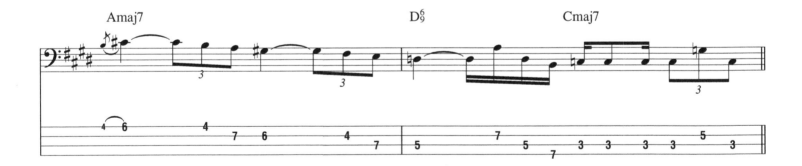

F

Emaj7

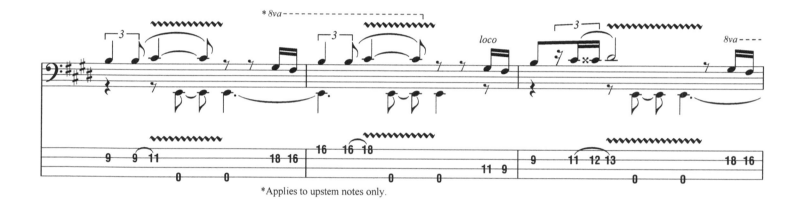

*Applies to upstem notes only.

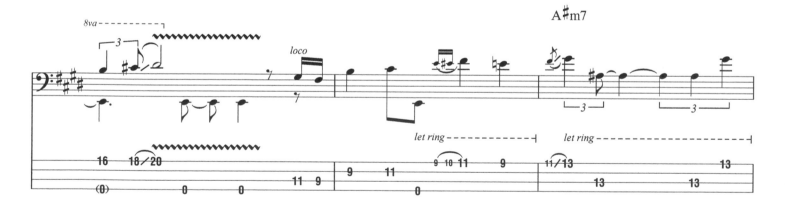

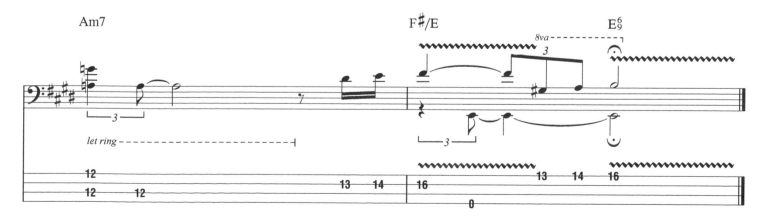

Dry Cleaner from Des Moines

Words and Music by Joni Mitchell and Charles Mingus

Verse

or-anges, three lem-ons, three cher-ries, three plums. I'm los-in' my taste for fruit __ watch-in' the

dry clean-er do it like Mi-das in a pol-y-es-ter __ suit. It's _____ all __ luck; __

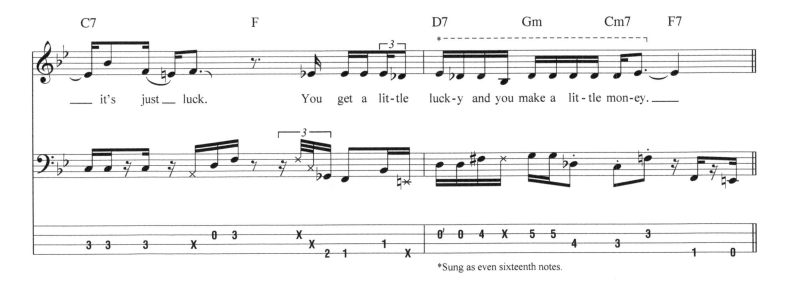

___ it's just __ luck. You get a lit-tle luck-y and you make a lit-tle mon-ey. _____

*Sung as even sixteenth notes.

Interlude

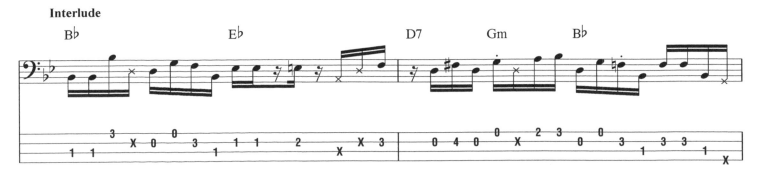

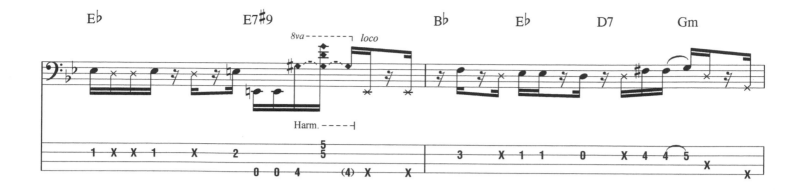

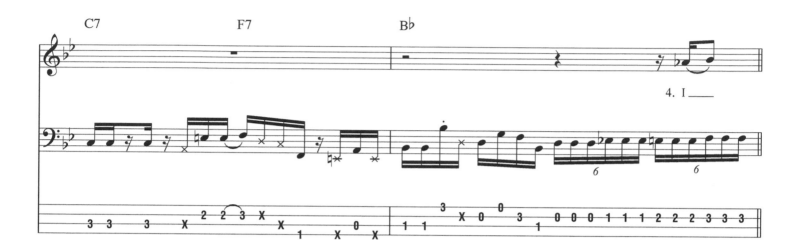

Verse

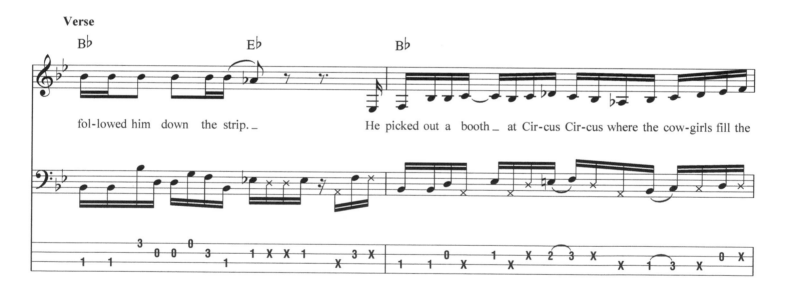

fol-lowed him down the strip. _ He picked out a booth _ at Cir-cus Cir-cus where the cow-girls fill the

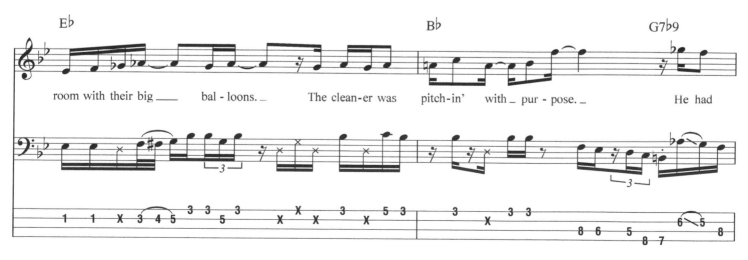

room with their big ____ bal - loons. _ The clean-er was pitch-in' with _ pur - pose. _ He had

Di-nos and Pooh Bears and li - ons pink and blue there. He could-n't lose there.

Interlude

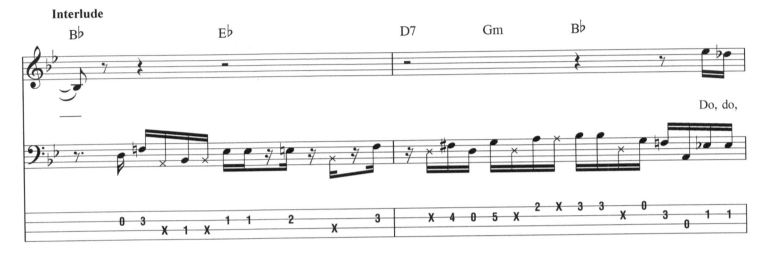

Do, do,

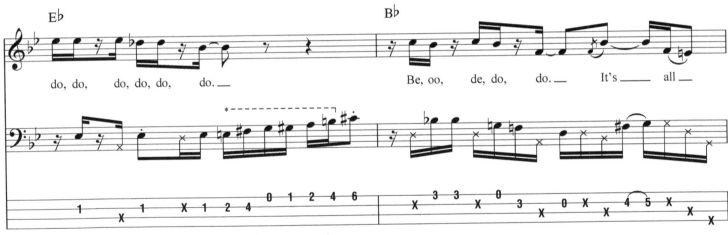

do, do, do, do, do, do. Be, oo, de, do, do. It's all

*Played as even sixteenth notes.

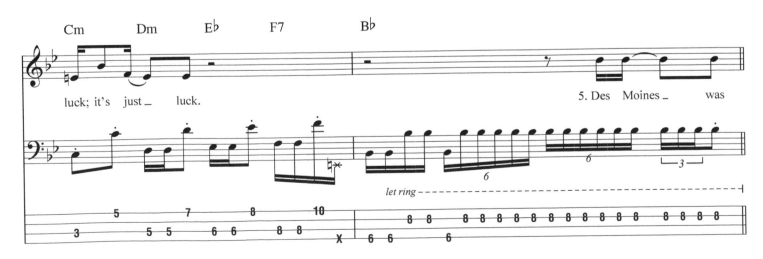

luck; it's just luck. 5. Des Moines was

let ring

Verse

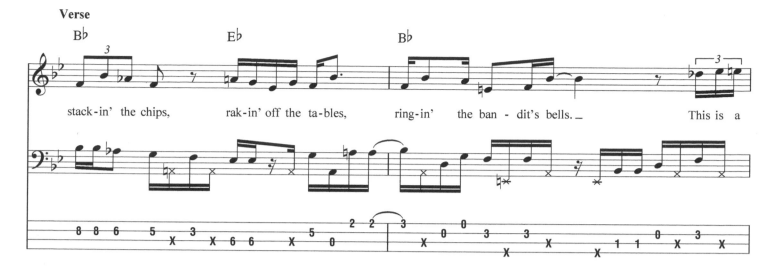

stack-in' the chips, rak-in' off the ta-bles, ring-in' the ban-dit's bells._ This is a

sto-ry that's a drag_ to tell_ in some_ ways since I lost ev-'ry dime I laid on the line. But the

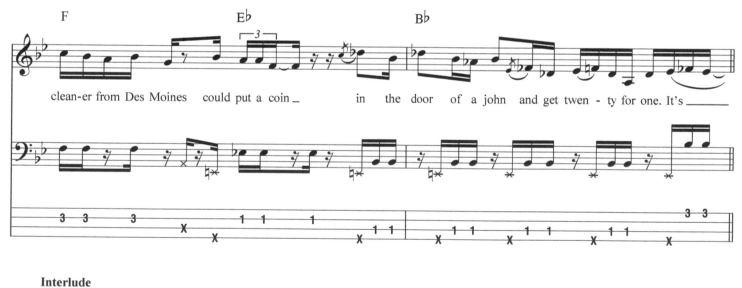

clean-er from Des Moines could put a coin _ in the door of a john and get twen-ty for one. It's _____

Interlude

___ just l - luck.

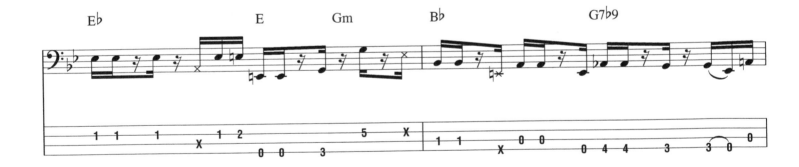

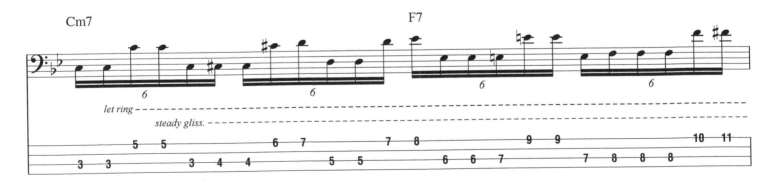

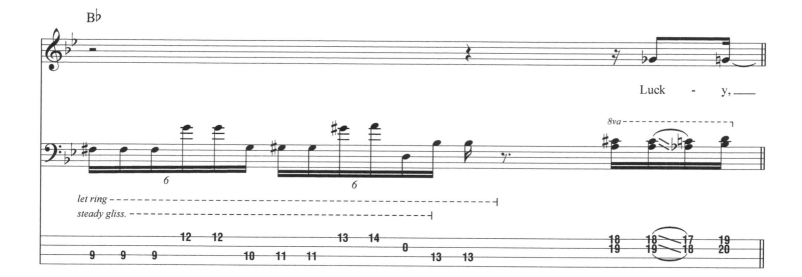

Outro

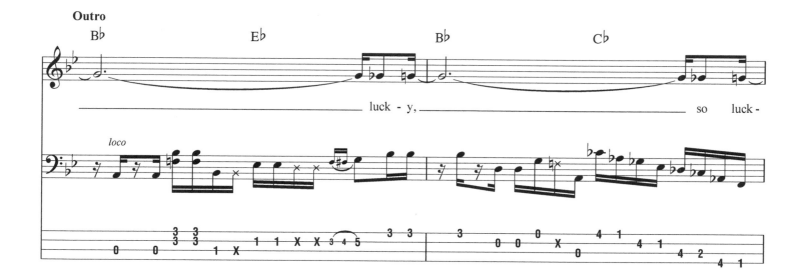

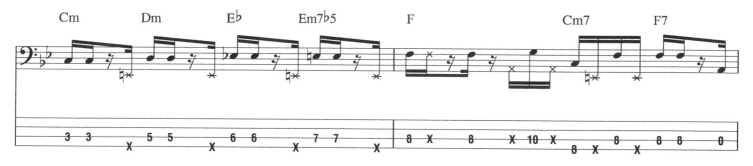

That cat's — got luck.   That cat's — got luck.

That cat's — got luck.   That cat's — got luck.

That cat's — got luck.   Real-ly

luck-y.   (Luck-y.   Luck-y.   Luck-y.

Luck-y. Luck-y.   Luck-y.   Luck-y.   Luck-y.   Luck-y.

Luck-y.   Luck-y.   Luck-y. Luck-y.   Luck-y.   Luck-y.   Luck-y.

Luck - y.   Luck - y.   Luck - y.   Luck - y.   Luck - y.)

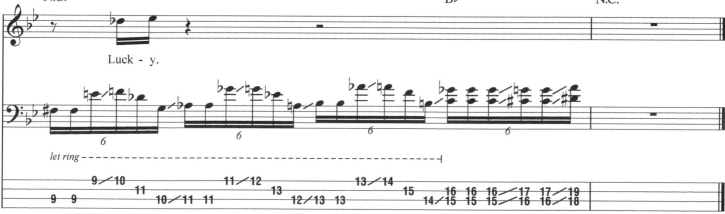

N.C.   B♭   N.C.

Luck - y.

let ring -

Harlequin

By Wayne Shorter

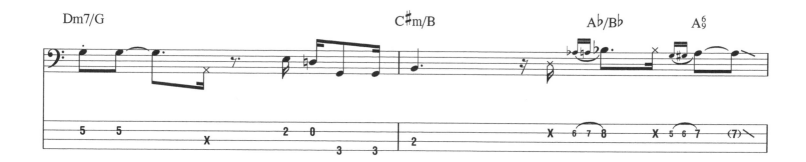

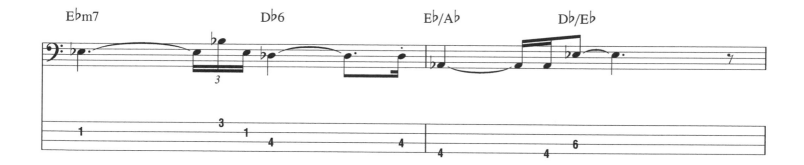

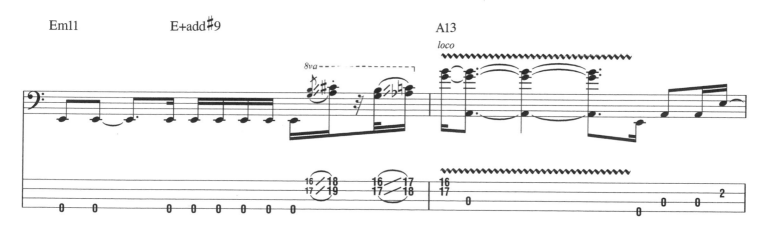

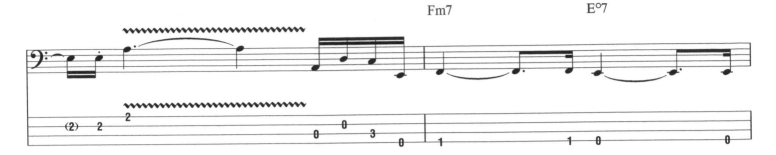

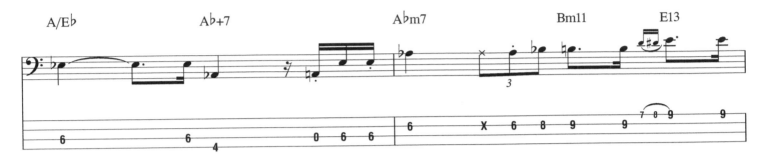

D

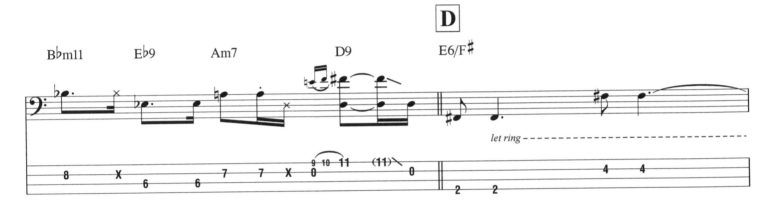

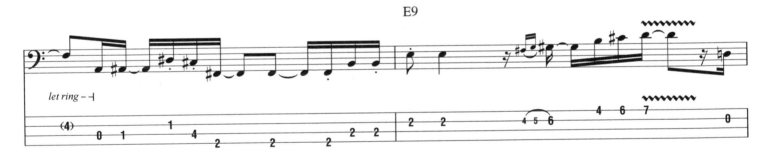

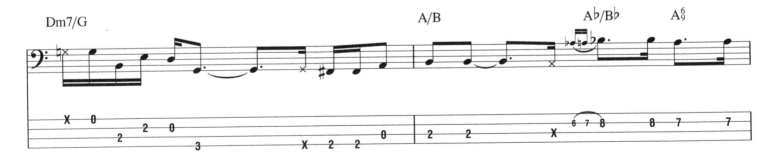

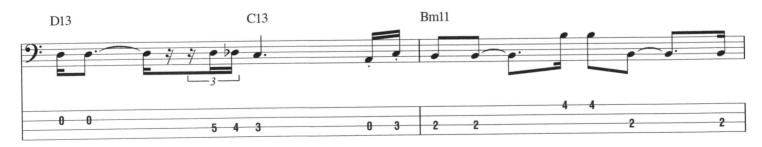

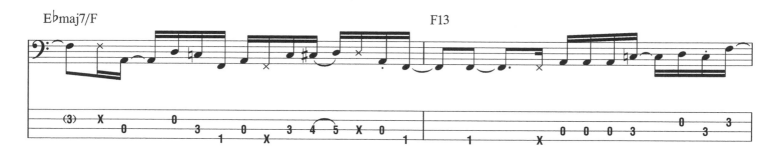

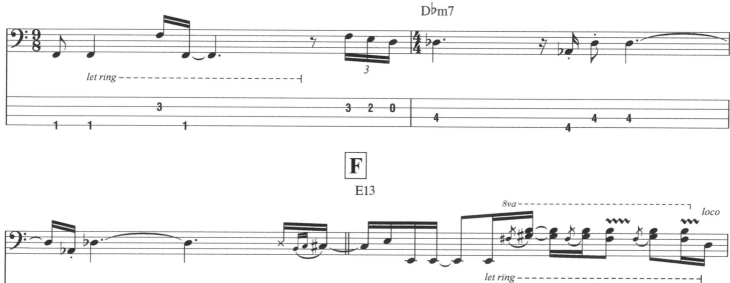

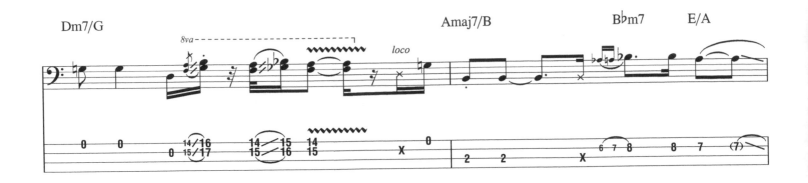

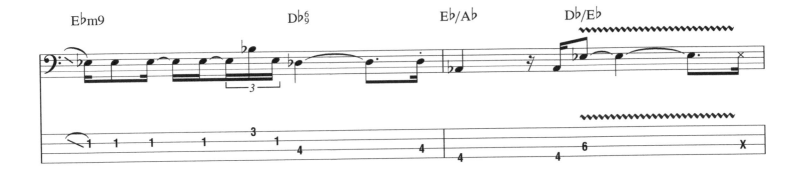

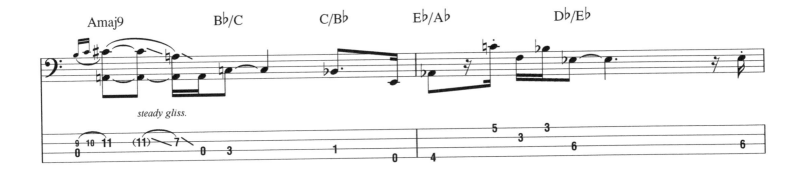

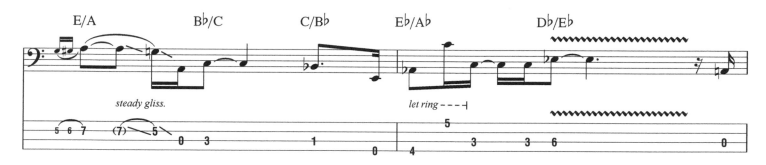

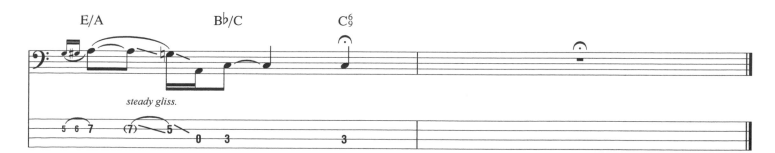

Teen Town

By Jaco Pastorius

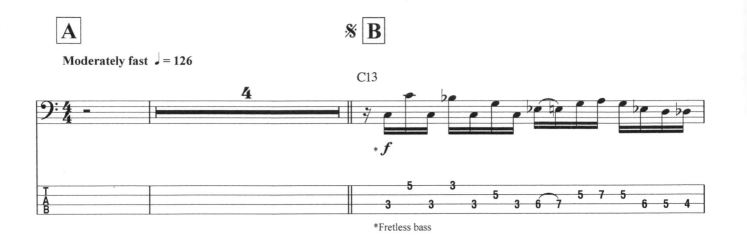

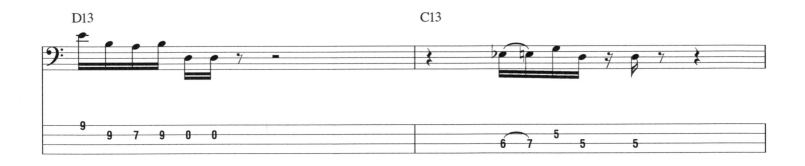

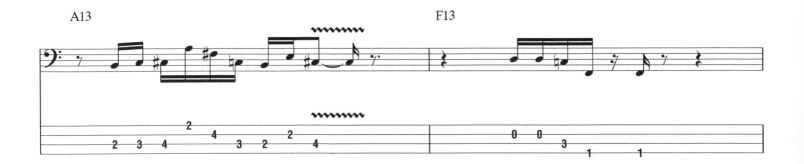

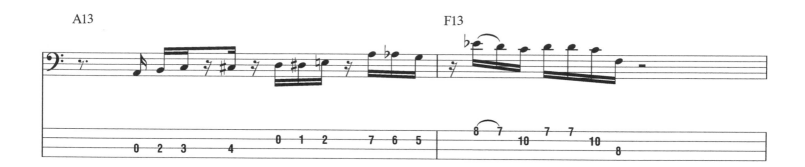

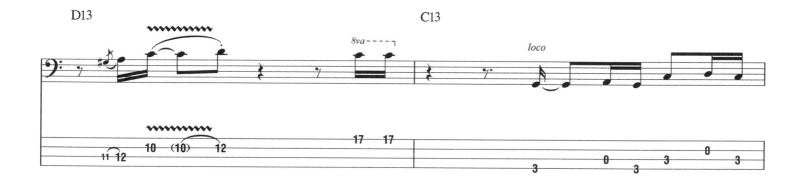

D.S. al Coda ⊕ **Coda**

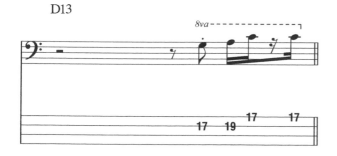

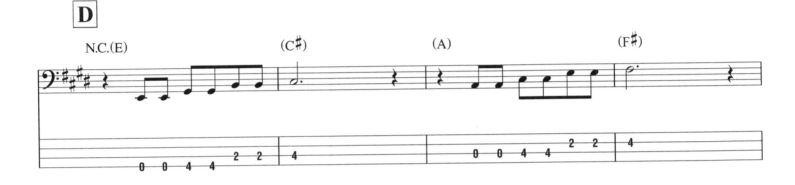

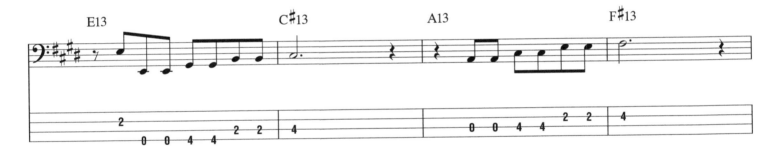

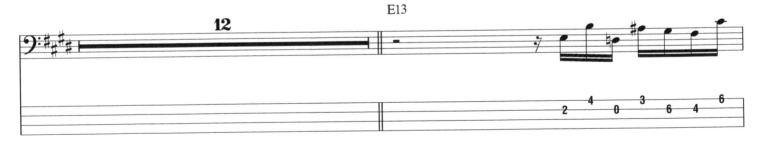

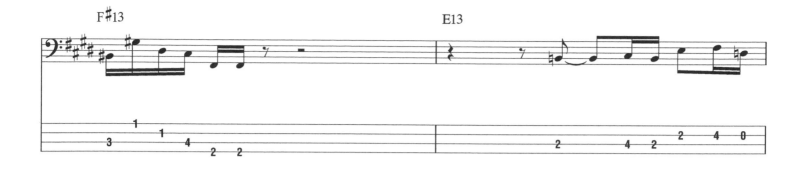

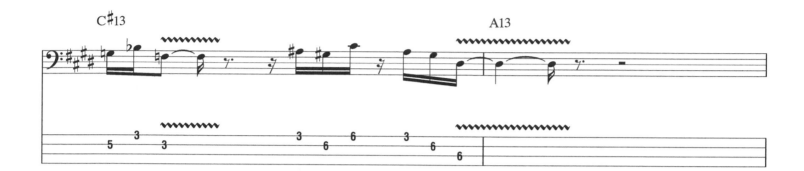

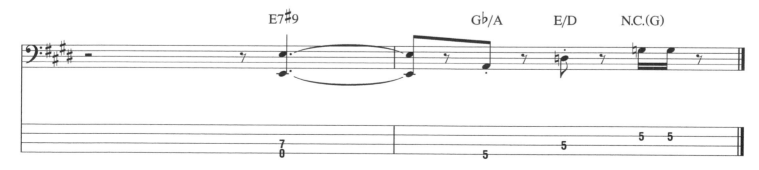

4 A.M.

By Herbie Hancock

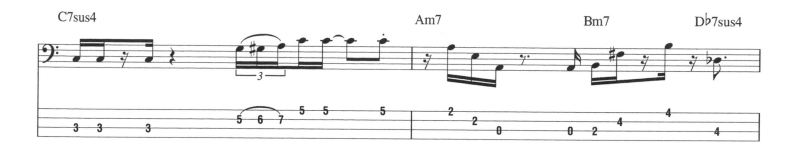

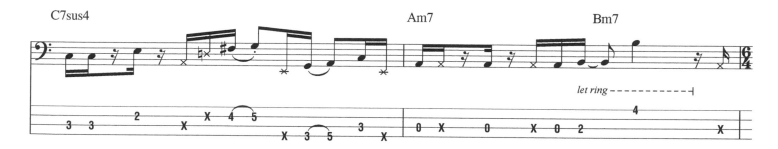

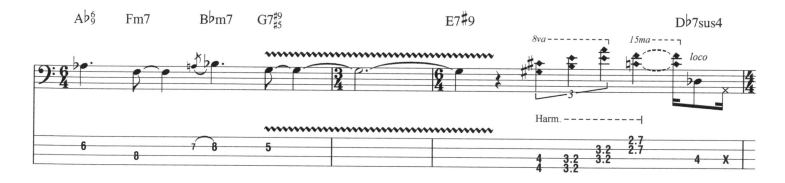

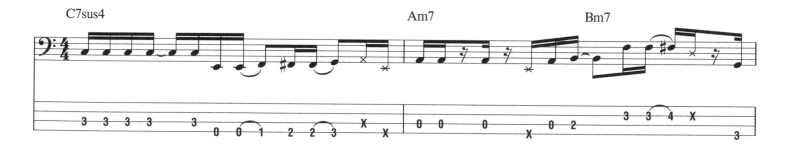

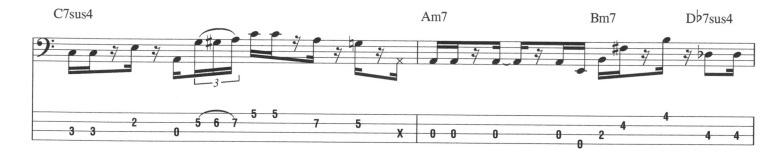

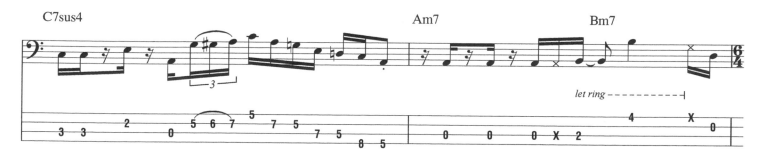

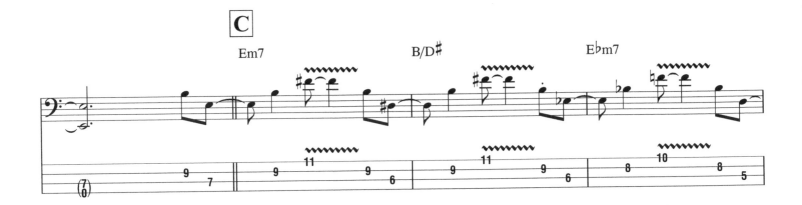

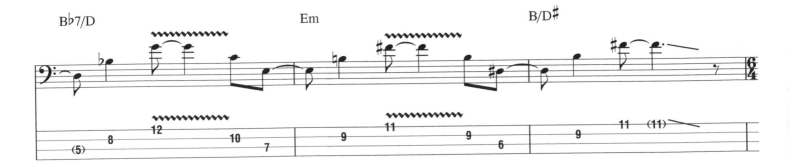

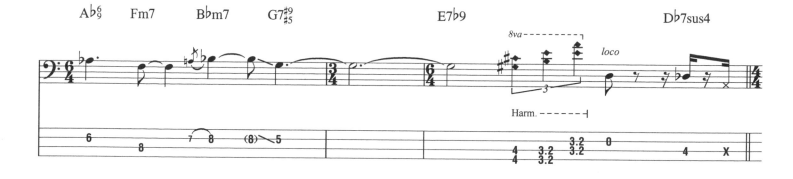

D

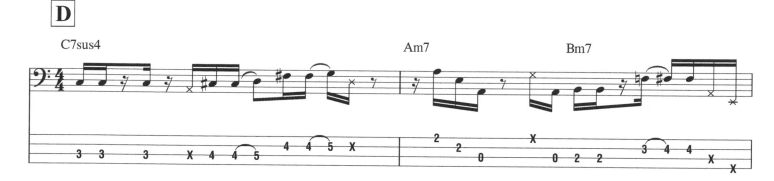

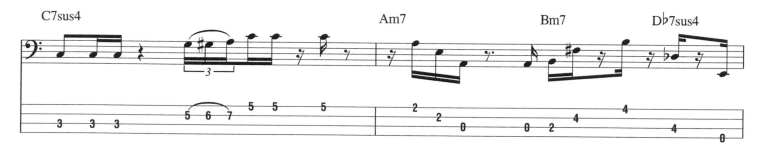

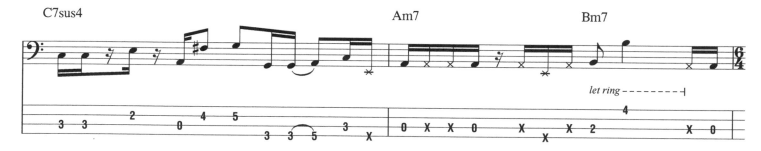

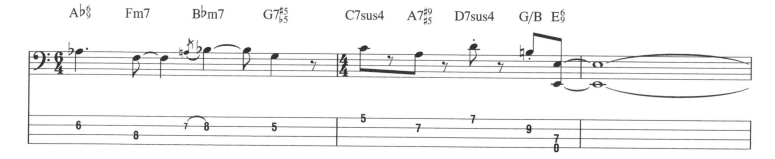

E

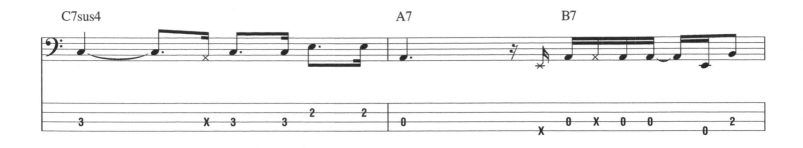

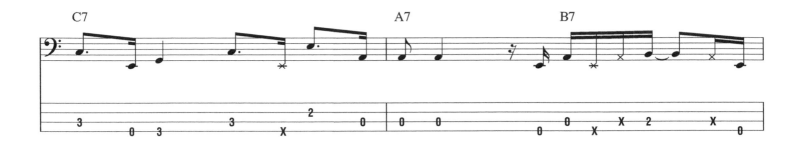

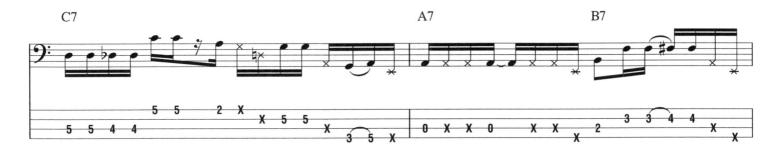

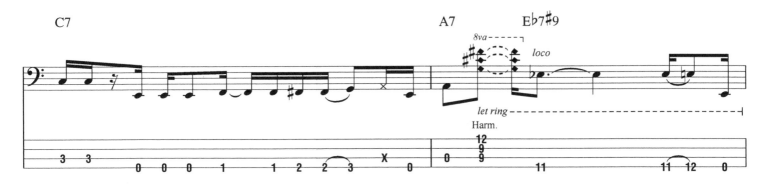

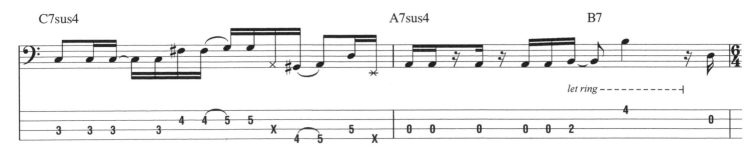

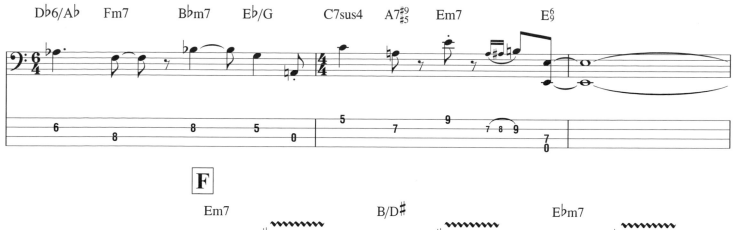

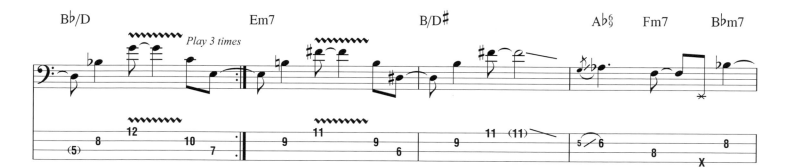

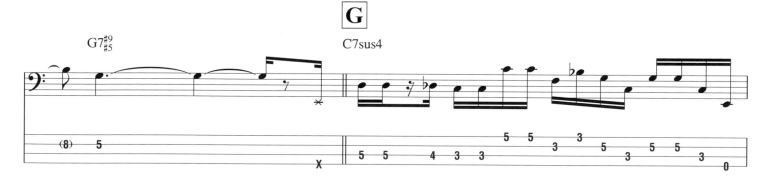

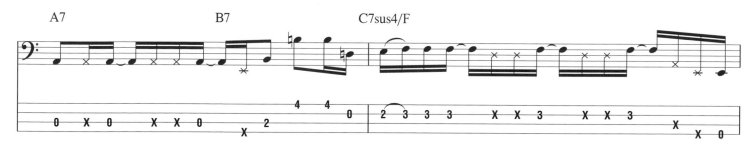

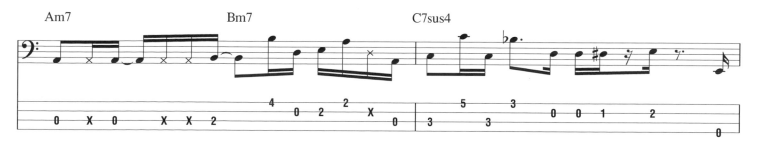

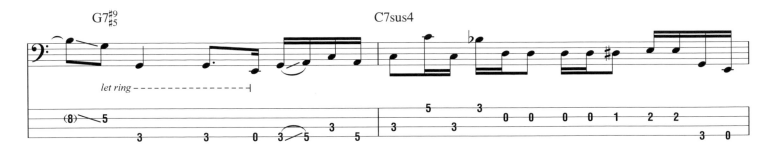

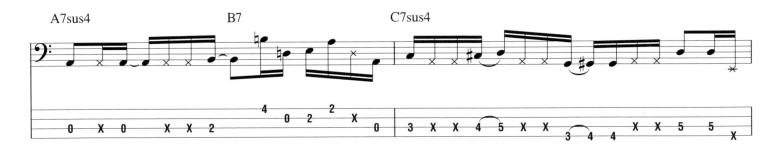

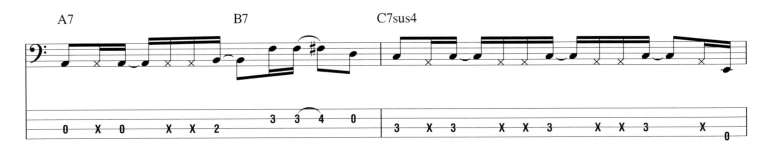

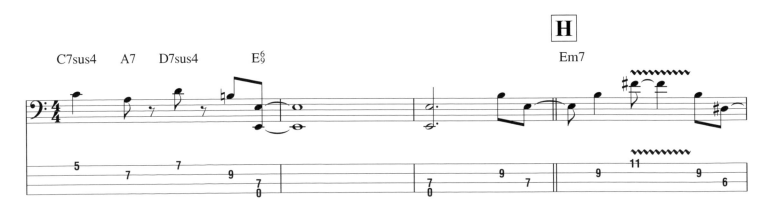

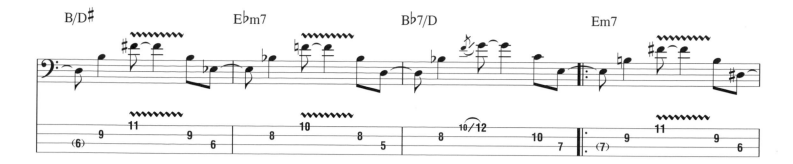

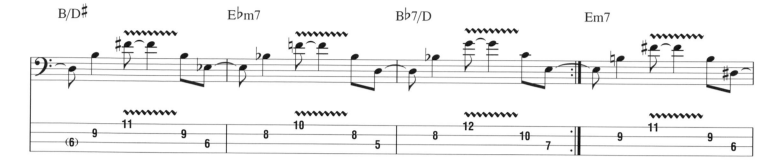

I

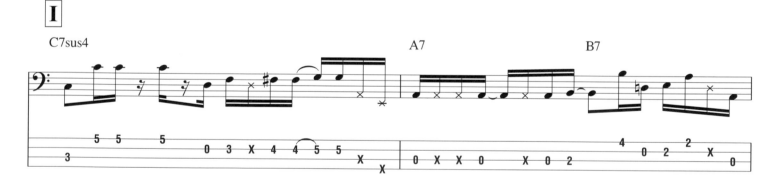

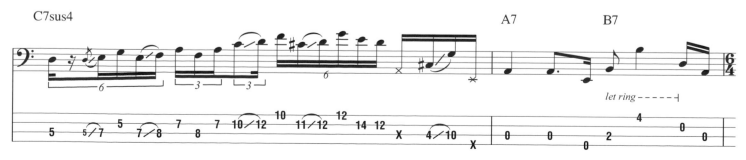

J

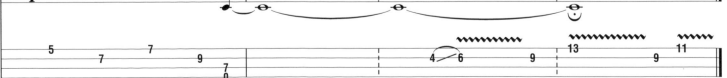